MARCS of a Disciple

Robby Gallaty

Published by Replicate Resources, Hendersonville, Tennessee.

ISBN-13: 978-0692691472 (Replicate Resources)
ISBN-10: 0692691472

Library of Congress Cataloging-in-Publication Data.

Printed in the United states of America.

Unless otherwise noted, Scripture quotations are from Holman Christian Standard Bible®, Copyright © 1999, 2000, 2002, 2003, 2009 by Holman Bible Publishers. Used by permission. Holman Christian Standard Bible® and HCSB® are federally registered trademarks of Holman Bible Publishers. Scripture quotations marked ESV® are taken from The Holy Bible, English Standard Version® (ESV®), copyright © 2001by Crossway, a publishing ministry of Good News Publishers. Used by permission. All rights reserved.

To order additional copies of this resource, write to Replicate Ministries; 3031 Long Hollow Pike; Hendersonville, TN 37075; email info@replicateministries.org, or order online at www.amazon.com

To every disciple of Christ who is leaving a lasting legacy on the hearts of men and women through disciplemaking.

"What you have heard from me in the presence of many witnesses, entrust to faithful men who will be able to teach others also."

2 Timothy 2:2

CONTENTS

FOREWORD

In his book *Growing Up*, Dr. Robby Gallaty defined disciple-making as "intentionally equipping believers with the Word of God through accountable relationships, empowered by the Holy Spirit, in order to replicate faithful followers of Christ." He examined how to root ourselves in Christ in *Firmly Planted*. In *Rediscovering Discipleship* he presented the philosophy of disciple-making and its trail through history. But once the process of disciple-making have been uncovered, many of us begin asking a new series of questions: How can I gauge the spiritual maturity of someone I am investing in? How can I measure my own spiritual maturity? How can we tell whether someone is growing into the image of Christ?

We can measure a budget's success by comparing income and expense. We can measure a baseball team's success by tracking its wins and losses. We can measure a film's success by its popularity at the box office. Unfortunately, however, looking for numbers to demonstrate a believer's spiritual maturity just doesn't work. A focus on growing wide often results in a large number of people with ankle-deep maturity.

If you long for insight into your own spiritual growth or the spiritual growth of those you invest in, you are in for a treat. In *Marcs of a Disciple*, Dr. Gallaty shares an effective method for measuring exactly this. After more than 30 years of making disciples, I have found both his practice of disciple-making and the method you are about to discover for measuring the spiritual growth of those disciples to be absolutely true. These chapters are filled with truth and practical insight that you will immediately be able to apply both to yourself and to those you mentor. I whole-heartedly commend this valuable resource!

Tim Lafleur

Pastor for Campus Development

Long Hollow Baptist Church

INTRODUCTION

Two months before the end of my discipleship group, I challenge each member to pray about potential people they can approach about meeting for twelve to eighteen months in a D-group (discipleship group). The names are then listed on a board (or in a notebook) for two reasons: 1. To pray for each person by name, and 2. To visually display the multiplication process before our eyes (Figure 1 illustrates how one of my D-groups reproduced from 5 to 30 in one generation).

Johnny	Jeff	Dallas	Corey	Robby
Victor	Jeremy	Gary	Ron	Richard
Nathan	Bobby	Ty	Brad	Jim
Kyle	Sam	Bryan	Brandon	Rick
Aaron	David	Jason	Kevin	Monte
Steve	Mark	Jose		Chad
	Corey			

Figure 1

As I was about to launch one of my D-groups, a contractor/home builder posed a question to me, **"How will we know if our groups are effective? How will I know if the group is growing spiritually? Basically, how can I tell if our discipleship model is working?"** He wanted a scorecard to gauge success.

Have you ever asked these questions? If so, you are not alone. Many disciple-makers regularly struggle with these issues. While attendance and baptisms are easily counted, measuring the spiritual maturity of our people is not quite so simple. To make matters worse, an unfortunate reality of our day is that pastors are graded on how big their churches are and not how mature their people have become. Sadly, the American church has adopted business metrics to grow churches rather than biblical methods for growing disciples. Mike Breen summed up this sentiment by saying, "If you seek to build a church, you rarely produce disciples, but if you seek to make disciples you always get the Church."[i]

Eugene Peterson commented on how Western churches have historically gauged their effectiveness when he wrote:

Pastors of America...are preoccupied with shopkeepers' concerns—how to keep the customers happy, how to lure customers away from competitors down the street, how to package goods so that customers will lay out more money. Some of them are very good shopkeepers. They attract a lot of customers, pull in great sums of money, and develop splendid reputations. Yet, it is still shopkeeping; religious shopkeeping to be sure, but shopkeeping all the same. The marketing strategies of the fast-food franchise occupy the waking minds of these entrepreneurs; while asleep they dream of the kind of successes that will get the attention of journalists.[ii]

This church consumer mentality often leads to measuring the wrong markers or placing the emphasis of our strategies and systems on incorrect endeavors. Jesus' model for growth (discipleship) revolved around spending time with twelve men who would go on to do the same. Likewise, He explicitly calls every believer to make disciples in Matthew 28. If making disciples was His method for growing the church and reaching the world, shouldn't it be ours?

Growing Members Not Just Ministries

Unfortunately, making disciples is easier said than done. Applying a standard against which we can measure them is ambiguous at times, for it is not simply a matter of measuring how tall a plant grows, how much fruit a tree produces, or how deep its roots descend into the dirt.

Some frequent questions when launching a discipleship strategy are, "What are our goals? How can we gauge our effectiveness?" Discipleship, after all, is messy, it's organic, and it's much harder to quantify than simply tabulating how many people attend an event. Ultimately, the spiritual development of its church body is paramount to any Bible-believing church. **If we begin to focus on the depth of our disciples, God will take care of the breadth of our ministry.**

When a church focuses on growing its members deep rather than just wide, it is a conscious decision to go against the grain of an amusement-based, low-commitment church culture where success is determined by how many people show up for a service on Sunday morning. Dallas Willard rightly stated, "Instead of *counting* Christians, we need to *weigh* them."[iii] It is time to change the metric by which we gauge the effectiveness of our churches. Exponential growth happens within the confines of a discipleship group or D-group.

What's a D-group?

A D-group is a gender exclusive group of three to six people meeting together for a season of 12 to 18 months. The meeting place is insignificant: it can be someone's home, a restaurant, a break room at work, or at church. In order to fulfill its purpose and be profitable, each meeting must be focused on the disciple-building activities discussed throughout this book.

Before beginning any disciple-making relationship, expectations between the mentee and the mentor must clearly be discussed and understood. Both parties must sign the disciple-making covenant, agreeing to take the relationship seriously. Stress the importance of attending weekly meetings and completing all assigned work as you distribute the document. A *Personal Faith Inventory* will serve as a platform for discussion during the group's first meeting. (Visit **www.growingupchallenge.com** to download the *Covenant* and *Personal Faith Inventory*.)

The entire discipleship process is outlined in *Growing Up: How to be a Disciple Who Makes Disciples*. At some point during the process, each participant should lead a session. Without incorporating this step, many may feel ill equipped to replicate the process and later lead their own group.

The discipleship process is completely reproducible, and it is designed to be replicated in the lives of others. Jesus commanded us to go into the world and make disciples (Matthew

28:19). He followed this command with instructions for developing disciples: "teaching them [future disciples] to observe all that I have commanded you" (Matthew 28:20).

As you study and grow, remember that you are not merely learning for your own benefit, but also for the benefit of others. Again, you must take notes. How else will you pass on the information you have learned?

Guiding others in their walk with Christ is a joy that is overlooked by many. The first and foremost way to make disciples is to become a disciple, and the only way to teach others effectively is to continue as a lifelong learner. We are closest to Christ when we are doing what He has commanded us to do, and the best way to learn is to teach. However, many are unsure of metrics for gauging success in a d-group.

MARCS of a Healthy D-group

The maturity of a believer is hard to measure, is it not? How do you measure the depth of an individual? Are there certain elements that are essential for determining whether or not a discipleship group (D-group) is healthy? I believe that there are. The MARCS of a healthy discipleship group are guideposts for determining the health of your discipleship ministry and disciplining relationships. Each element is meant to be incarnational not just duplicate-able, meaning the principles identified from the ministry of Jesus will work in any church size, age, culture, context, or maturity level. The MARCS are:

- **Missional**
- **Accountable**
- **Reproducible**
- **Communal**
- **Scriptural**

Don't just read through this book. Use it as a measuring stick to determine the health and effectiveness of the D-groups in your church and personal life. Reference it throughout the year to gauge maturity in your own life and make course corrections along the way. Remember, you can't expect what you don't inspect. Spiritual growth will not happen accidentally. Jesus didn't leave the maturity of his disciples to chance; neither should we.

Disciple-making Resources

Here are some disciple-making resources to assist you on your journey:

- *Growing Up* (A Practical Manual for Making Disciples)
- Firmly Planted (Basic Growth Objectives for Every Believer)
- *Bearing Fruit* (The Fruit a Disciple Produces)

- *Foundations: A 260 Day Bible Reading Plan for Busy Believers*
- *Rediscovering Discipleship* (The Why and How of Making Disciples)
- **replicate.org** (Weekly Discipleship Articles, Videos, and Materials)
- **discipleshipblueprint.com** (A two-day experience design to equip you with a model for making disciples)

Chapter 1

MISSIONAL

*"**Go, therefore**, and make disciples of all nations, baptizing them in the name of the Father and of the Son and of the Holy Spirit, teaching them to observe everything I have commanded you. And remember, I am with you always, to the end of the age." Matthew 28:19-20*

Missional Mindset

The first measure of a disciple's spiritual growth is whether or not they possess a missional mindset. When most people see the word "missional" they envision a missionary—someone who has left his or her home to travel to a faraway country with the message of the Gospel. It frequently conjures up images of someone leaving behind comfort and familiarity to venture into the unknown under the direction of the Holy Spirit.

When a missionary is on the field, they adopt a different mindset than when they are back home. They think, speak, and act differently; everything they do is pointed toward the ultimate reason they are in this new setting. A missionary is *always* on mission. The same is true when you embark on a mission trip.

Unfortunately, there is no rule that states the only place to be "on mission" is on the mission field. As a matter of fact, every follower of Jesus should be on mission. A missional disciple is not a person with a passport in a foreign land. They are everyday believers who are intentional in a familiar town, constantly on the lookout for divine appointments, and always willing to heed teachable moments.

"Missional living" has been misunderstood by some. For example, it includes evangelism, but mere evangelism does not constitute missional living. Evangelism can be as brief as an event or a presentation; missional living, rather, is a *mindset*.

It is not a place to go, it is the priority of one's life. We are missional by living intentional where God has planted us.

Jesus expected his followers to be on mission, but they wouldn't necessarily be called missionaries. Occasionally, they were sent out to do ministry but would eventually return to their hometown. In reality, most of their mission work occurred during their everyday lives. Jesus gave them the cut-and-dry outline for living missionally in Acts 1:8, where he told his followers, "You will receive power when the Holy Spirit has come on you, and you will be My witnesses in Jerusalem, in all Judea and Samaria, and to the ends of the earth." He expected them to do the work of ministry during the course of everyday life.

Jesus' outline for how to live missionally applies to our lives today. Before giving you practical ways to live on mission, let me explain the two requirements that are necessary for missional living.

Missional Living Requires a Supernatural Power

The first part of Jesus' mandate for missional living contains a promise: each disciple will receive power from the Holy Spirit. The word for "power" in Greek is the word *dunamis,* which is found in nineteen of the twenty-seven New Testament books. Additionally, *dunamis* is the Greek root of our word dynamite—the explosive kind of dynamite. But sadly, many have made the mistake of reverse-applying this connection when

4

trying to describe the type of power that the Holy Spirit brings.

It is a mistake that many are prone to make because of how powerful an image it provides. The major problem with comparing the power of the Holy Spirit with the power of dynamite is that dynamite was not invented until 1866. Neither Jesus nor his disciples were thinking of dynamite when Jesus mentioned the words of Acts 1:8.

Jesus had an entirely different kind of power in mind. Consider the thoughts of author D.A. Carson on this matter: "Dynamite blows things up, tears things down, rips out rock, gouges holes, and destroys things. The power of God of which Paul speaks is often identified with the power that raised Jesus from the dead, aiming for the wholeness and perfection implicit in the consummation of our salvation."[iv]

When Jesus spoke of power to his disciples, he was not envisioning the power to tear apart and destroy life, but the power to provide life and raise human beings from the dead. This kind of power comes solely from the Holy Spirit.

Mark, the gospel writer, wanted us to know that Jesus was filled with the same kind of *dunamis* to accomplish his purpose. In first few chapters of Mark's gospel, he unfolds the extent to which Jesus, filled with this power, possesses all authority:

- Jesus holds authority over wild animals. (1:13)
- Jesus holds authority over the angels. (1:13)
- Jesus holds authority to teach Scripture. (1:22)
- Jesus holds authority over sickness. (1:34)
- Jesus holds authority over the devil. (1:34)
- Jesus holds authority over sin. (2:9)
- Jesus holds authority over the Sabbath. (2:27)

• Jesus holds authority to give authority to others. (2:27)

Later, Jesus demonstrates authority over nature as he calms the sea (Mark 4:35-41) and walks on water (Mark 6:45-52), all for the purpose of teaching his disciples he has all authority on earth. This exact authority is what makes his final commission in Matthew 28:18-20 a *great* one! "All authority in Heaven and on Earth has been given to me" so "go, therefore, and make disciples of all nations..."

But it doesn't stop there. The Holy Spirit, the guarantee and seal of our future inheritance in heaven (Eph. 1:13-14), is the same Spirit that Jesus mentions in Acts 1:8. He will indwell believers with the same *dunamis* Christ promised. Anyone indwelt with the Holy Spirit possesses the power of God.

Twelve Untrained Men

It is fascinating to consider whom Jesus chose to carry out his mission. Look at the list of disciples he entrusted to deliver the greatest message ever delivered:

Andrew—an introvert

Peter—a man with a foot shaped mouth

James and John—both desired to call down fire on the Samaritans

Matthew—an IRS Agent

Simon the Zealot—a card-carrying political activist

If I were selecting a team, these men are not my first draft picks. Jesus bypassed the theological centers of Jerusalem, the wealthy cities of Tyre and Sidon, and the upper class establishment of Jericho. He chose men who weren't the smartest or most sophisticated. The motley crew He assembled was not wealthy or politically savvy.

However, Jesus chose them for the same reasons that he chose you and me. He wanted to demonstrate that without Him we are nothing short of a train wreck, but *with* Him we can do all things. Without Him, we are incapable; with Him, we are capable.

The most common excuses I hear from people as to why they aren't involved in making disciples is that they are fearful of the unknown or don't know possess enough biblical knowledge. The truth is that most Christians would admit the same thing. We are all full of insecurities and doubts. However, God can use any of us. A healthy dependence upon God is necessary for investing in others. Do not underestimate the power of the Holy Spirit and the impact of the Word of God. You are not in this by yourself; you are not standing alone. Jesus is with you every step of the way.

Missional Living Requires a Single-Minded Plan

Before unpacking Acts 1:8, we must first examine the verses that come immediately before it. Without the context, a text can be distorted to say any variety of things. Before we begin to examine Acts 1:8, look first at verse 3. Though it is just one verse, it provides a timeline for us. For forty days, according to verse 3, Jesus taught his disciples about the Kingdom of God. Forty days of Kingdom discourse was clearly enough to get the disciples excited. In verse 6, they ask Jesus directly. "When are You going to set this Kingdom up?"

If we imagine being in their shoes, we probably would have asked something similar. Remember, the political climate in the first century was rocky, especially for Jews. For this group of disciples, it was even more tumultuous. A twisted uprising in Jerusalem ended with the death of their Master.

So, after forty days of watching their risen Messiah perform miracles and teach about His coming Kingdom, they were presumably still focused on an imminent return, expecting to come out on top, perhaps by overthrowing their Roman oppressors. They were ready to inaugurate the Kingdom Jesus spoke so often about.

Acts 1:7 records the first part of Jesus' answer to them. In essence, he says, "Don't worry about when I'll set that up." Jesus hadn't left yet, and still the disciples were inquiring about his return. We are in a similar situation, but the truth remains for us just as it did for them. Let us not spend all of our time looking for the second coming of Christ and neglect the last command of his first coming. Such a mindset will lead to the regret of wasted years.

Next, He outlines a plan for gospel expansion in verse 8: "You will receive *power* from the Holy

Spirit and you will be My witnesses." What Jesus did in his answer to the disciples was shift their focus and understanding about the nature of the Kingdom of heaven. It is not just some future event that will commence with trumpet blasts; it is a present task given to his followers who are to be witnesses for Him.

A witness is, essentially, something that points toward something else. A witness in court is someone who testified about an an event for the purpose of illuminating the truth. A billboard is a witness of sorts. It doesn't draw attention to itself, but to the image it displays. A mirror doesn't draw attention to its glass, it draws attention to what the glass reflects. Witnesses are largely invisible. They are part of the bigger picture (no pun intended). When Jesus says that we are to be his witnesses, this is the exact idea he is communicating.

Being a witness does not insinuate knowing all biblical truths, possessing an arsenal of bulletproof arguments, or having more Scripture memorized than your neighbor. A witness is one who reflects the glory of God. The question a witness should ask is not, "Am I good, strong, trained, or smart enough to be a witness?" It is, rather, "Do I want to be used by God?"

Being a witness does not just include going overseas. The disciples began in Jerusalem and worked out from there. They didn't just rush to the "ends of the earth." **Do not be so quick to cross the ocean to share the gospel with the nations that you neglect crossing the street to share the gospel with your neighbors.**

You Can't Argue with a Changed Life
When someone is on mission, they possess something of a missional mindset. These

individuals understand that where they are is not their final destination, but rather they are where they are for another more important reason. A missional mindset affects almost every aspect of a person's life. Being on mission affects how we dress, how we act, how we spend our time, where we eat, and the words we speak. St. Francis of Assisi is paraphrased as saying, "Go into the world and preach the Gospel, and if necessary, use words." (Modern scholars don't believe he actually said this.) Unfortunately, this saying is not biblically supported. What should be said is, "Go into the world and preach the Gospel, and *since* it is necessary, use words." If we are disciples on mission, our speech will reflect our lifestyle.

In Romans 10:15, Paul did not say, "Faith comes by *seeing*, and *seeing* through the Word of Christ." He said, "Faith comes by *hearing*, and *hearing* through the Word of Christ" (emphasis mine). And before he says that, notice the case Paul builds for sharing with *words*:

> How then will they call on him in whom they have not believed? And how are they to believe in him of whom they have never *heard*? And how are they to *hear* without someone preaching? And how are they to preach unless they are sent?[v]

It is absolutely crucial we speak the Gospel. A family member told me, "I don't need to share the Gospel with my co-workers. They know I'm a good person who lives with integrity. They can see that." My response was, "What they need to hear, though, is *why* you're a 'good person.'" People around you need to understand that Jesus is the difference that made a difference. The fruit that we bear should point people to Christ, but it simply cannot stop there. It is crucial to be ready

15

at all times to provide a defense for the hope that is within us.[vi]

For some, the idea of sharing the Gospel is simply terrifying. Perhaps you are fearful of being asked a question you won't have an answer or you'll be laughed at for what you believe. Remember, in addition to the gospel message, believers wield a potent weapon: their personal testimony. Anybody whose life has been changed by professing faith in Christ possesses a built-in mechanism for sharing the Gospel.

A believer should be able to share his or her testimony at any given moment. A testimony is simply the story of what Christ has done in your life. An effective testimony is not a difficult thing for you to write out. It should be about five minutes to present and has just three parts:

1. This is what my life was like before I came to Christ.

2. This is what happened that changed my life (how I came to Christ).

3. This is my life after God saved me.

Your success is not in how many people got saved because you shared it with them. Results are measured by how many people *heard* the Gospel because you spoke it to them. **Success in evangelism is in the sharing, not the saving.** It is difficult to argue with a changed life.

How to Live on Mission

In the context of a D-group, missional living happens when the participants are held accountable for fostering intentional friendships and engaging in lifestyle evangelism. The most overlooked mission fields are the ones we spend the most time in: our workplaces, our neighborhoods, and in the presence of our family members.

A surprisingly effective way to live missionally is to make the conscious effort to befriend people with no strings attached. Do not require people to do something for you or return favors. Ask questions about your friends' lives without expecting them to ask you in return. Listen without waiting for your turn to talk. It is remarkable what kind of difference listening more and talking less does to improve the relationships around you.

Dale Carnegie, author of *How to Win Friends and Influence People*, understood this principle well when he wrote, "You will do more in the next two weeks showing a sincere interest in others than if you spend the next two years trying to get others interested in you."[vii] The philosopher Immanuel Kant called it treating others like they are ends in themselves, rather than just means to our own end.

The people around you should not be viewed as projects to complete or boxes to check for proof of a super-spiritual life. Instead, you should live out the benefits of the Gospel and genuinely display the love of Christ—not as objects of attention, but as witnesses to God. **A person isn't a goal; a person is a precious soul for whom Christ died**.

A disciple living missionally will also pray for those around them. Feel free to ask about their struggles and triumphs, about how best to build each other up, and how you can best pray for them. By treating those around you as ends in themselves, you are modeling missional living and setting up future Gospel conversations at the same time.

Divine Appointment Calendar

You may be entirely on board at this point, but wondering how you could ever make time for missional living. The fact is that we are all very busy cramming meetings, ball games, and dinner menus into every corner of our wakefulness we can muster. Let's face it, we are terrible at making room for divine appointments. However, once we've gotten the hang of speaking the Gospel whenever we can, and living missionally with the people around us on a regular basis, we begin to realize that believers in Christ are always on mission because we do not cease being the Church.

Reggie McNeal, in his book *Missional Renaissance*, said, "Missional followers of Jesus don't belong to a church. They are the church. Wherever they are, the church is present. Church is not something outside of themselves that they go to or join or support; it's something they are. The missional church is not a *what* but a *who*. When we think of church in the *what* mode, we focus on something that exists apart from people, something 'out there' that people join and attend and support. We try, then, to build great churches, believing that this is God's primary strategy to engage the world. Inevitably, this preoccupation leads to discussions of how we can 'do church' better. Simply thinking about the church in the *who* mode, focuses on what it means to be the people of God. The central task is developing great followers of Jesus, believing that God has created people to demonstrate his redemptive intentions to the world in and through them."[viii]

For the believer in Christ, there is no separation between the sacred and the secular because we are *always* missionaries, no matter where we are.

Some of us are good missionaries where we are. Most of us are not.

If we aren't careful, we may miss divine appointments God schedules into our lives because we aren't looking around often enough to see them. We miss people at the gas station, chance meetings at Target, or opportunities at Starbucks. Adjusting a busy life to free us up for those little moments does not require drastic steps. The steps could be as simple as:

- Lingering longer in the driveway before going into your home.
- Hanging around a few minutes extra in the break room.
- Inviting lost friends over to have dinner with you.
- Serving in a local homeless shelter occasionally.

- Leading after school tutoring at a school that needs help.
- Investing time in community events.
- Getting involved in prison ministry.
- Letting your neighbor borrow something of yours.
- Volunteering in your church nursery or to set up for an event.

These are only suggestions. The possibilities are endless. Doing simple things can open up incredible doors for intentional ministry.

Most who go on overseas mission trips find themselves thinking differently, acting differently, sharing the Gospel differently, and conducting everyday life differently. But there is no reason a believer should have to carry a passport, pack luggage, and hop on a plane in order to be missional. The trick is thinking like a missionary in our everyday lives. It could start with something as simple as living like a missionary in your home around your own family, being a missionary among our coworkers, or viewing your next trip to the coffee shop through a missional lens.

The two keys to missional living are *intentionality* and *availability*. Until we are those two things, evangelism is just an event or sales pitch. Missional living motivates us to wake up every single day and realize we are on mission with God.

So, slow down and look around.

Divine appointments are everywhere.

Chapter 2
ACCOUNTABLE

*"Go, therefore, and make disciples of all nations, baptizing them in the name of the Father and of the Son and of the Holy Spirit, **teaching them to observe** everything I have commanded you. And remember, I am with you always, to the end of the age." Matthew 28:19-20*

One of the fastest ways to waste money in marketing is through what is called "hope marketing." Hope marketing is the practice of advertising a product with the hope it reaches the desired audience or produces the desired results. If this kind of marketing is done without split testing, web copy evaluation, or advertisement analysis, it will dissolve an advertising budget faster than an Alka Seltzer in water.

Sadly, the same mentality is prevalent in many discipleship groups. If a D-group's leader fails to set expectations or have an effective method to gauge the spiritual growth of his or her members in the group, the participants may be tempted to become lazy and disengaged. **What doesn't get measured doesn't get done**. We can rephrase it in a positive manner: **What gets measured gets accomplished**.

As we are learning to gauge the spiritual depth of a D-group by looking at its MARCS, we come next to one of the most crucial aspects of any discipleship growth: accountability.

Even though the word "accountability" is not found in Scripture, the concept is seen everywhere. For example, consider Adam and Eve (Gen. 3:8-19), Samuel and Saul (1 Sam. 13:8-14), Nathan and David (2 Sam. 12:1-14), and Jesus and Peter (Matthew 16:21-23). In each of these cases, someone's actions are being held in check by God, a fellow worker, or a teacher. Chuck Swindoll described accountability as "opening one's life to a few carefully selected, trusted, loyal confidants who speak the truth—who have the right to examine, to question, to approve, and to give counsel."[ix]

Even for the believer who thinks he or she doesn't need to be accountable to anyone, Scripture dictates otherwise. Each of us is accountable in three areas: God (Heb. 9:27), spiritual leaders (Heb. 13:17), and to other believers (Prov. 27:17). Accountability is integral to a D-group because it directly lends itself to deeper connections with each other and with God. Accountability is what sets the D-group apart from a Sunday school class or a small group, for issues that cannot be discussed in the context of a large gathering with mixed genders are revealed in this smaller group.

Rod Handley, the former president of FCA, said, "Accountability will not remove sin or keep you from sin, but it helps you become aware of your sin, and helps you focus your attention back on Christ. Being accountable (to another person) takes honesty, and if it doesn't exist it will be a meaningless experience!"[x]

Accountability gives someone the right to speak into your life with truth in love, call out sin that needs to be addressed, and hold people to the promises they make. Every single one of us needs accountability in our lives if we wish to grow. Ecclesiastes 4:9-12 explains why.

> Two are better than one because they have a good reward for their efforts. For if either falls, his companion can lift him up; but pity the one who falls without another

to lift him up. Also, if two lie down together, they can keep warm; but how can one person alone keep warm? And if someone overpowers one person, two can resist him. A cord of three strands is not easily broken.

In the context of this passage, Solomon had just explained that compulsive working is wrapped in vanity, both of which are a misfortune and a miserable task. He uses this section to transition into the case that meaningful relationships are more valuable than worldly riches. While many people have used these verses to support the institution of marriage or collaboration in the workplace, it can be used just as easily in the context of disciple-making.

Accountability Supports Our Work

Ecclesiastes 4:9 echoes the beginning of verse eight, which reads, "There is a person without a companion, without even a son or brother, and though there is no end to all his struggles, his eyes are still not content with riches." Solomon paints a pitiful picture of the lone wolf mentality. Loneliness and perpetual dissatisfaction seem to haunt him, especially in light of the uplifting and joyful exaltation of journeying with others.

Still, the key term to pick out in this section is *companion*. A companion is someone who is a partner, joined through a covenant bond of friendship and fellowship. "It is not good for man to be alone," God explained in Genesis 2:18. We weren't created for solitude, but rather for deeply connected, intentionally accountable community that legitimately looks out for and works with one another. Notice the promise that Solomon highlights in verse nine for community: good reward. Whether this is a physical, material, or spiritual blessing depends entirely on the situation; the fact remains that God declared for us to work with one another.

You will never find a Jewish Book of World Records. Why? Jewish men would never imagine competing against his brother. Companionship, not competition, is crucial for living the Christian life. "In a day of tarnished leaders, fallen heroes, busy parents, frantic coaches, arrogant authority figures, and egg-headed geniuses, we need mentors like never before—we need guides, not gods. Approachable, caring souls who help us negotiate our way through life's labyrinth."[xi] In a discipleship relationship, course correction does not come from a position of authority—like a boss or a parent—but from a position of mutual respect and love.

Accountability Strengthens Our Walk

"For if either falls, his companion can lift him up; but pity the one who falls without another to lift him up. Also, if two lie down together, they can keep warm; but how can one person keep warm alone?" (Ecclesiastes 4:10-11).

Solomon provides a practical image for what a discipleship relationship accomplishes. If you fall into a metaphorical pit while walking alone, there will nobody there to get you out of it. But if you are walking consistently with two to four other believers who are constantly looking out for each other, speaking truth into one another's lives, and helping each other steer clear of obstacles, if one falls down, there are companions to help him back to his feet.

We learn these principles at an early age. When small children go on field trips, they often employ the *buddy system*. If you can remember, the buddy system works with simplicity. Every child is paired with a buddy so that at any time they can determine whether one child is missing, hurt, or in trouble. They sit with their buddy on the bus, experience the field trip together, and then return together at the end of the day. As disciples, our walks are to be the same. We should always be looking out for someone else as someone else looks out for us.

In the early 90s, a television commercial is remembered for an iconic one-liner that is, unbeknownst to the makers, a perfect example of why accountability is so crucial in a Christian's walk. In this commercial, a number of people have encountered problems in their homes when no one is home. The memorable line comes from Mrs. Fletcher, who has tumbled to the floor in her kitchen. Luckily for her, she remembered to don her medical alert pendant that morning, and is able to press the button while famously yelling, "I've fallen and I can't get up!" The vigilant dispatcher on the other end of the call says, "We're sending help immediately, Mrs. Fletcher."

Our accountability companions respond exactly the same for us. When we come across peril, when we are knocked down and unable to pick ourselves up, and when difficult times come, our D-group companions will lift us back on our feet.

Traveling in Israel when Solomon penned these words was be a treacherous endeavor. Wild animals lived by the sides of the road and robbers lay in wait to steal whatever goods a traveler might have been carrying. Perhaps even more dangerous than other people or savage beasts were the elements. Temperatures soared during the day and plummeted at night. One way to keep warm on a long journey was with blankets, but these blankets occupied precious room and added weight to the animals carrying the travelers' supplies. The easiest way to keep warm during these cold middle-eastern nights was to travel with a companion. At night, this traveling companion could provide crucial body heat to battle the rapidly dropping temperatures.

It is easy to grow cold as a believer. Bitterness and anger can creep in to our daily routines without us noticing and without watchful eye of someone holding us accountable. One of the hallmarks of the D-group is the built-in accountability, which is essential for spiritual growth.

Accountability Safeguards Our Well-Being

Ecclesiastes 4:12 highlights the dangers of traveling in ancient Israel: "If someone overpowers one person, two can resist him. A cord of three strands is not easily broken." Not only would companions keep one another warm, they would also ward off and defend against predators or robbers. There is strength in numbers—a lesson revealed all throughout Scripture and Jesus' teaching. In the parable of the Good Samaritan, for example, the beaten man is cared for and nursed to health by someone who helped him. Traveling companions provide company on the road, warmth at night, and a helping hand to restore us.

This passage does not merely stop at extolling the virtues of traveling with a partner, however. Notice the progression of support. In verse eight, Solomon demonstrates an unhappy solitary person. In verse nine, he moves from that solitary man to a much better scenario of two people traveling together. In verse 12, however, he states that three is better than all of the above.

Ancient rabbis have commented on the use of a cord in this context: "This cord was used to imply the advantages and greater strength of three persons functioning as companions, particularly in the matter of living and transmitting Torah or the Bible.[xii]" When three people are present for the transmission of God's Word—which happens to be a function of a D-group—there are two other people to provide balance, perspective, and stability that is not present if a Christian is trying to live a solitary Christian life.

Once, D.L. Moody was attempting to explain to a prominent figure in Chicago his need for Christian community. They were seated in the man's parlor on a chilly winter evening. Coal was lit in the fireplace. Moody sat as the man explained that he was capable of being just as good a Christian outside the church as he could be in it. He could read the Bible on his own, pray, even sing songs by himself if he must. Moody listened patiently without saying anything as the man presented his case for being just fine on his own.

Once the man was done, Moody stepped to the fireplace, took the tongs out of the rack, picked a blazing coal from the fire and set it on the mantle by itself. In silence, the two watched it smolder and die out.

The man looked at Moody and said, "I see your point."

In the same way a burning coal will extinguish if separated from other coals, a man or woman who is disconnected from the care and accountability provided by companions will watch the heat of his faith glow regressively more faint.

Meet Together for Encouragement

The author of Hebrews wrote about two further benefits of meeting with others: promoting good works and encouraging one another. Hebrews 10:24-25 says, "And let us be concerned about one another in order to *promote* love and good works, not staying away from our worship meetings, as some habitually do, but *encouraging* each another, and all the more as you see the day drawing near" (emphasis mine).

To promote something means to *spur on* or *motivate*. Sometimes, the word used here can be translated as *to irritate* or *to provoke*. The idea is simple: sometimes we have to be reminded to live for Christ when we get off course. The second benefit of community is to provide us with encouragement. To encourage someone is to come alongside and strengthen them with instruction, admonition, warning, or consolation.

Every one of us gets beaten down throughout the week, tempted by the flesh, or discouraged by the world. We desperately need encouragement, and a weekly D-group provides a consistent avenue for this.

Michael Billester once gave a Bible to a humble villager in eastern Poland with simple instructions: commit the Bible to memory. When he returned a few years later, he learned that two hundred people had become believers in that village. When the group gathered to hear him preach, he suggested that before he spoke he would like each person to quote some verses of Scripture. One man rose and said something to the tune of, "Perhaps, brother, we've misunderstood you. Did you mean verses or chapters?" Billester was astonished. "Are you saying that there are people here who can recite entire chapters of the Bible?" That was precisely the case. In fact, 13 of them knew half of Genesis and the books of Matthew and Luke. Another had committed all of the psalms to memory. Combined, the two hundred believers knew virtually the entire Bible.[xiii]

The fact is that the majority of believers have not taken the responsibility to read and memorize the Word as seriously as these believers did. The main reason is that no one has held you accountable to do so. With like-minded people speaking encouragement (and perhaps prodding us along) to memorize Scripture, for example, we'll be exponentially more likely to hide God's Word in our hearts.

Scripture memory is a scalable measure of growth that is easy to observe and track. But such black-and-white, observable criteria comes with the unfortunate risk of becoming legalistic. When anything we do flows from a self-absorbed desire to check boxes and not from an abundant love for God and His word, we can lose sight of the reason we practice spiritual disciplines in the first place.

Accountability must be couched in grace. Avoid narcissistic, self-improvement regimens that turn grace into law. Any good in us is a result of the finished work of Christ on the cross. Our striving for holiness is a motivation *from* something not a motivation *for* something. Salvation drives us to obedience. We obey because Christ first obeyed the Father. We serve because Christ came to serve and not be served. We study the word because Jesus was the Word who became flesh among us. **Remember, the goal of accountability within the confines of a D-group is always devotion never duty.**

Confess Sin and Pray Together

Jesus' half-brother James wrote, "Therefore, confess your sins to one another and pray for one another, so that you may be healed. The urgent request of a righteous person is very powerful in its effect" (James 5:16). Within the confines of a trustworthy group of men or women, you will feel comfortable confessing your faults to one another over time. Notice James's incentive for praying for one another: healing. Whether someone is struggling with sexual sin, sickness, financial worries, relational issues, or emotional strains, everyone benefits from confessing his or her shortcomings to trusted individuals.

The enemy desires for us to keep our sin hidden. Sin thrives in darkness, where it can fester, grow, and grip our lives. The larger a sin grows, the harder it is for us to let it go. What confession of sin does is thrust that sin out into the light where it can be dried up and suffocated. **Sin will always take you further than you want to go, keep you longer than you want to stay, and cost you more than you want to pay.**

I would be willing to bet if you are not experiencing victory over sin, you're battling it alone. Dietrich Bonhoeffer emphasizes the dangers of isolation: "Sin demands to have a man by himself. It withdraws him from the community. The more isolated a person is, the more destructive will be the power of sin over him."[xiv] Finding individuals whom we can trust is not an overnight process—it takes time to develop the kind of trust where deep secrets can be shared with confidence and confidentiality.

Bear One Another's Burdens
Paul wrote in Galatians 6:1-2, "Brothers, if someone is caught in any wrongdoing, you who

are spiritual should restore such a person with a gentle spirit, watching out for yourselves so you also won't be tempted. Carry one another's burdens; in this way you will fulfill the law of Christ." We saw earlier in this chapter that having companions, in the context of a D-group, provides fuel to keep the fire burning in the form of accountability and encouragement. In this passage, Paul speaks of the tone for such conversations: gentleness.

Speaking from a man's perspective, we are taught from an early age to be macho and tough. Men aren't supposed to show their emotions or wear their feelings on their sleeves. This is not the attitude of a disciple of Christ, however, because it is not the attitude of Christ. Jesus was never described as "macho" or "tough." However, he was called "meek" and "mild." Jesus was compassionate, caring, and even cried over a close friend (see John 11). A disciple should exemplify His same manner of life.

Disciples carry each other's burdens. They hold each other accountable, share their feelings, and learn from one another. In this community, real relationships are valuable and trust is an utmost priority.

But still, the most important and readily available accountability group that someone can find is in the home. If you have not given your spouse a free pass to speak into your life, you are missing out on one of the greatest benefits of marriage. From the beginning of our marriage, I have asked Kandi, my wife, to speak freely and openly into my life. Although some of the comments are hard to swallow at times, I know she has my best interest in mind. This practice provides an opportunity to model appropriate behavior and cultivate an environment of discipleship in your home.

Discipleship is not just limited to the congregation of a church, either. Pastors too should give a small group of trusted friends the right to speak into their lives. Welcoming insights, critique, and helpful comments from a team of trusted believers not just in their personal lives but also about sermons they preach might sting at times, but it is an indispensable step in becoming a Christ-honoring, Bible-based leader. Accountability is almost non-negotiable if we desire to:

- Read the Word consistently
- Memorize Scripture
- Work hard at the office
- Avoid lustful attitudes, tempting thoughts, and inappropriate conversations
- Spend time with our families

- Share the Gospel with lost people
- Show up consistently for a weekly meeting knowing that hard questions may be asked
- Live with integrity

Consider one final word from the late Dr. Howard Hendricks, former professor at Dallas Theological Seminary, about the necessity of disciple-making:

After more than forty-five years of working with men in terms of mentoring relationships, I can tell you without reservation that the men who are making the greatest impact for God in this generation are men who have placed themselves under the tutelage of other godly men. If you care about making any kind of difference with your life—in your work, with

your family, in your community, in your faith—
then find someone who can help you grow
and realize your life goals.

Chapter 3
REPRODUCIBLE

*"Go, therefore, and **make disciples** of all nations, baptizing them in the name of the Father and of the Son and of the Holy Spirit, teaching them to observe everything I have commanded you. And remember, I am with you always, to the end of the age." Matthew 28:19-20*

If Jesus had said in Matthew 28:19, "Go, therefore, and make *converts* of all nations," the church would be doing an okay job, for it has been the primary goals of many churches throughout history. The problem is that Jesus didn't instruct us to make converts. He didn't even encourage us to build church buildings. Instead, He commanded something specific: "make disciples of all nations."

I heard a pastor say once, "If the Lord would call a meeting of the board the way corporations do, and if the Lord would hang on the wall a progress chart the way corporations do, and if He were to explain that chart to us and show us how the graph is going down the way corporations do, He would have every right to fire us the way corporations do." As tough as this pill is to swallow, there is some truth to it. When I asked my friend Bill Hull for the first step a person must take to make disciples, he responded, "They must repent for not making disciples up to this point."[xv]

The problem is not lack of resources; it is a fundamental misunderstanding of the mission at hand. After all, we have money—God has given us all of the resources in the world to carry out His commission. It is in your pockets and bank accounts. We have the manpower—we have people, churches, Christian schools, top-of-the-line seminaries. We have the mandate—*Go and make disciples*. We have the method—within our mandate is the expectation of replication. Had those who heard these original words not replicated, we certainly wouldn't be here today talking about them.

Discipleship without Reproduction is not Biblical Discipleship.

When I speak at churches or conferences on discipleship, people frequently stop me to talk after the sessions. One lady in Orlando stopped me and said, "Pastor Robby, I have enjoyed everything you have said about discipleship. But I want you to know that we have been making disciples for years; we call it Sunday School." At first, I was taken aback by her sincerity. I asked one question that caused her to pause, "How many generations of reproduction have you seen in the Sunday School classes?"

God gave us a picture of the disciple-making process all the way back in the Garden of Eden. The processes of multiplication, replication, and reproduction are as old as the Old Testament. They are as old as mankind. Genesis 1:27 says, "So God created man in His own image; He created him in the image of God; He created them male and female."

From the beginning, God instilled three principles of multiplication, replication, and reproduction into everything that mankind does. First, He created us to bear the very likeness of Himself. He created us separate from the rest of the sentient life He put on the Earth. He imprinted us with His divine fingerprint that each person bears either well or poorly. Second, He entrusted us to preserve His Word. One of the first instructions

He gave Adam and Eve was a command. He expected them to guard His Word, though they did it irresponsibly. Third, He empowered us to multiply on the earth. He gave Adam the responsibility and ability to subdue the earth, knowing the first couple, left to their own devices, would be unable to do it alone. With this power came the ability to procreate and multiply, giving humans a broader reach both geographically and chronologically.

The kind of replication expected of Adam and Eve was the same as it is today: to produce children according to the values of mom and dad. The same goes for the discipleship process.

You will reproduce what was introduced to you.

Many discipleship relationships throughout Scripture bear the hallmarks of how yours should function today. Think of Moses and his disciple Joshua, which multiplied through the generations to raise up leaders for the nation of Israel. Elisha had a school of prophets that replicated to affect future generations (Amos 7:14). Jesus selected twelve followers to be His disciples, who then carried out His command to reproduce themselves. Paul made disciples everywhere he went—Timothy, Titus, Silas, Mark, and Luke, to name a few.

In fact, in his letter to Timothy, Paul penned a passage that impacted Billy Graham's personal ministry. He comments:

> One of the first verses of Scripture that Dawson Trotman, founder of the Navigators, encouraged me to memorize was 2 Timothy 2:2. This is like a mathematical formula for spreading the gospel and enlarging the church. Paul

taught Timothy; Timothy shared what he knew with faithful men; these faithful men would then teach others also. And so the process goes on and on. If every believer followed this pattern, the church could reach the entire world in one generation! Mass crusades, in which I believe and to which I have committed my life will never finish the Great Commission; but a one-to-one ministry will.[xvi]

The passage that Dr. Graham mentioned, 2 Timothy 2:1-2, is Paul's church growth strategy. It has absolutely nothing to do with buildings, worship teams, budgets, or Sunday School, or programs, but everything to do with the people that make up a body of believers. It contains crucial information for those involved in the discipleship process about how to replicate future generations. Paul instructed his son in the faith Timothy to:

> Be strong in the grace that is in Christ Jesus. And what you have heard from me in the presence of many witnesses, commit to faithful men who will be able to teach others also.[xvii]

Abide in the Power of Christ

Just before giving Timothy this exhortation to replicate his faith, he mentions two people by name who have decidedly not remained faithful to the mission that was entrusted to them: "This you know: All those in Asia have turned away from me, including Phylegus and Hermogenes" (2 Tim. 2:15). Placing the context of verses 2:1-2 in contrast with those who abandoned their faith accentuates Paul's command to Timothy. It reads something like, "Don't be like those people;

rather, be strengthened by the Spirit and reproduce others like yourself."

Paul wants Timothy to tough it out. Not by his own strength. He must depend on the grace that Christ Jesus provides to accomplish the task. Timothy must realize there is an unending supply of grace that flows from the crucified, risen, reigning Christ. He will be empowered by the Holy Spirit to make disciples and so are we.

Timothy would have connected these dots easily. Earlier in the letter, Paul wrote, "Therefore, I remind you to keep ablaze the gift of God that is in you through the laying on of hands. For God has not given us a spirit of fearfulness, but one of *power*, love, and sound judgment." (1:6-7, emphasis mine). Paul reiterated it again just a few verses later: "Hold on to the pattern of sound teaching that you have heard from me, in the faith and love that are in Christ Jesus. Guard, *through the Holy Spirit* who lives in us, that good thing entrusted to you" (1:13-14, emphasis mine).

Without depending on the Holy Spirit, we run the risk of turning out like Phylegus and Hermogenes, abandoning the race they started. Living the Christian life without relying on God's grace is an exercise in futility. C

My friend Tim LaFleur says: "The Christian life is either easy or impossible. It's impossible if you try to do it in your own strength. It becomes easier as you allow Christ to work in and through your life." The grace of God sustains us both when we think we have everything under control and when we feel like we have no control. Therefore, we should wake up every morning asking the Lord to fill us with His Spirit in order to carry out his mission in our lives.

You may feel like you don't have what it takes to make disciples, lead a D-group, or totally invest your life in others. In all honesty, you're exactly where God wants you. When we depend on Christ, we minimize the risk of being puffed up with conceit and tripping over our own pride. Stay dependent upon God.

Accept the Principles of Christ

Timothy heard the message from Paul in the presence of many witnesses. The fact that many people were around when Paul was teaching him gives the message credibility. It verifies the weight of truth and authorizes its contents. Paul is, in essence, saying, "What I taught you can be proven by the testimony of other people." Men like Barnabas, Silas, John, Mark, and Luke could have vouched for him.

Not only did Timothy hear the things Paul taught him, he obeyed them. It is embedded in Paul's teaching just as it was in Christ's. The last part of Christ's Commission to His disciples was a call for them to teach their disciples to obey so they could turn around and make even more disciples.

The phrase "what you have *heard* from me" encapsulates both Paul's instruction and Timothy's action. Hearing is more than just listening. *Shema* is the Hebrew word meaning "to hear", and was almost always paired with an action, particularly in the Old Testament. Two examples are found in Deuteronomy.

"Now, Israel, listen to the statutes and ordinances I am teaching you to follow, so that you may live, enter, and take possession of the land Yahweh, the God of your fathers, is giving you." (Deut. 4:1)

"Moses summoned all Israel and said to them, 'Israel listen to the statutes and ordinances I am proclaiming as you hear them today. Learn and follow them carefully.'" (Deut. 5:1)

My mom would always tell me, "Listen to me. If you don't pick up these toys and bring them to your bedroom you're going to sit in timeout." I would continue playing for another ten, twelve, or fifteen minutes without a concern for her instructions. My mother would approach me again, saying, "Did you hear what I said?"

I heard her loud and clear, but I wasn't acting upon what she said. Hearing implies absorbing the information and obeying it.

Invest in the People of Christ

What Paul wants Timothy to do is simple: "What you have heard from me, commit or entrust to faithful men." *Entrust* is an imperative, a command. It means to place before someone, like setting a feast upon a table. It means to trust someone with something for safekeeping.

The most remarkable thing about the Gospel is that we guard it by giving it away. We protect the investment of those who have entrusted it to us by passing it along to others who will do the same. Safeguarding the Gospel is not storing it away by hiding it in a bank. We must replicate it to the next generation. **The Gospel came to you because it was heading to someone else.**

When someone invests a year or two in your life, you can never repay them; their investment is life-changing. But you *can* do something to demonstrate your gratitude. The greatest gift someone whom I have invested time into can give to me is to pay the investment forward.

Finishing the Task

With the vast number of Christians in the world today, we could finish the Great Commission without enlisting even one more person. We already have all the resources we need sitting in the pews or padded seats every week. If we repurposed our energy on growing those people deep as we do on growing our congregations wide, an unstoppable force would be in mobilized. But this requires a shift in thinking from our present paradigm.

Leroy Eims, in his book, *The Lost Art of Disciplemaking*, tells the story of a pastor who called him in anguish. The young man said, "My church is growing, seeing many people saved, baptizing more people than ever before, and increasing in number. However, I need someone who can do more than take sermons to shut-ins, pray after the service, take up an offering, manage a business meeting, manage finances, or teach Sunday school." As good as those things are, he needed people who would lead people to Christ, disciple them into maturity, and replicate the process.

The greatest problem we face today in the Church is the vast amount of undiscipled disciples. We've stopped at "what you've heard from me," and haven't "entrusted to faithful men who will be able to teach others also."

For so many years, we have made evangelism the chief end of our ministry. Christians have believed that if we get someone to repeat a prayer, sign a card, make a decision to follow Jesus, and come back to church, the work is finished. That is not the completion of our work. It is merely the beginning. Jesus never said, "Go make converts." He said, "Go make disciples." There is a big difference.

Would you ever visit at new church with your infant, locate the preschool department, and drop off your child to an empty room without any supervision? And as you're walking away toss a bottle onto the floor in front of your newborn child and say, "Feed yourself. I'll be back in a few minutes to get you"? Of course you wouldn't. That's crazy to even think about.

Unfortunately, we do this every week with newborn believers. We call it church. So many churches are filled with infant Christians who are unable to feed themselves. Dr. Herschel Hobbs rightly said, "The work of evangelism is never complete until the one evangelized becomes an evangelizer."[xviii]

It is not that we don't need evangelism. We most certainly need to reach as many lost people as we can with the Gospel. But let's not stop there. That is not the end of our ministry. It is merely the start of it.

Reproducing the Priority of Christ

The goal of Paul's instruction to Timothy, and to us, is to make disciples "who will be able to teach others, also." In this one sentence, Paul represents four generations of discipleship: Jesus instructed Paul, Paul taught Timothy, Timothy taught faithful men, and those men invested in others. The process does not depend on master teachers or expert lecturers; that is a faulty understanding of discipleship. Paul merely implies teaching after being entrusted with something. He expects you to pass on what you've learned. A disciple is a learner, a note-taker, but not just for himself—for those he is going to invest in.

For Jesus, reproducing disciples was not just important, it was the priority. If investing in others was not paramount for Him, He would have gone to Jerusalem as a teenager, claimed to be God, labeled a heretic and blasphemer, and sentenced to death. He still would have died, risen from the grave, and ascended into heaven for the sins of all those who would believe, but He didn't do that. He devoted three years of his earthly life to twelve men. **Jesus' life was just as important as his death.**

This truth is emphasized in John 17. This passage describes Jesus praying His final prayer to the Father before heading to the cross. In His prayer, Jesus made a declarative statement to His father, saying, "I glorified You on earth, having accomplished the work that You gave me to do" (John 17:4). God gave Him a task—that task was not just to die on the cross. Notice that Jesus told the Father that He accomplished the work He was sent for, prior to dying on the Cross. In this prayer,

Jesus never mentions miracles, multitudes, or programs. Rather, forty times He prays for His disciples. The task the Father sent him to complete was to invest in twelve men. **We can't expect to experience the ministry of Jesus and divorce ourselves from the model he implemented—disciple-making.**

John Wooden, former UCLA basketball coach, knew the importance of discipleship. Wooden taught basketball according to simple pedagogical principles, which he called the Whole-Part method. He would show them the whole and then break each element down. He followed his basketball instruction with four laws of learning; explanation, demonstration, correction, and repetition. This sounds awfully familiar to the instruction that Paul gave: "What you've heard from me (explanation) in the presence of many witnesses (demonstration/correction), entrust to faithful men who are able to teach others also (replication)."

Even though reproduction is the key, a D-group will never actually *want* to stop meeting in order to disciple new people. After a year, a group will develop a common bond of friendship. Why would anyone want to disrupt that? My first D-group of 4 began in 2006. After meeting for a year and a half, no one felt ready to replicate when I moved from Louisiana to Tennessee to pastor Brainerd Baptist Church. I remember the guys asking me, "What are we supposed to teach? What if I get asked a question that I don't know the answer to?"

I responded, "If you guys don't do it, who will?" They had no choice. Each accepted the challenge and have been investing in men ever since I left.

But in answer to their question, there are four qualities we aim to reproduce:

1. **Believers who are under the rule of Christ.** This comes from Matthew 28:19, "Teach them to observe all that I have commanded You" (emphasis mine). We aren't just communicating truth from God's word. We are holding people accountable to live it out.

2. **Believers who repeat the Word of God.** This comes from Deuteronomy 6:4-9, "Listen, Israel: The Lord our God, the Lord is One. Love the Lord your God with all your heart, with all your soul, and with all your strength. These words that I am giving you today are to be in your heart. Repeat them to your children. Talk about them when you sit in your house and when you walk along the road, when you lie down and when you get up. Bind them as a sign on your hand and let them be a symbol on your forehead. Write them on the

doorposts of your house and on your gates." We should recite the Bible in our homes, in our communities, at our workplaces, and to ourselves.

3. **Believers who reflect the image of Christ.** Paul explains: "We all, with unveiled faces, are looking as in a mirror at the glory of the Lord and are being transformed into the <u>same image</u> from glory to glory; this is from the Lord who is the Spirit" (2 Corinthians 3:18, emphasis mine). Another Scripture that highlights the point is Romans 8:29: "For those He foreknew He also predestined to be conformed to the <u>image</u> of His Son" (emphasis mine). The goal of spiritual growth is to be like Christ.

4. **Believers who replicate the process of Christ.** We want to create people who take what they've learned and teach it to others, who will teach it to others. The gospel came to you because it was heading to someone else.

Imagine your doctor calls you in this week to go over some test results. He tells you that you have three years to live. If you knew that the time clock of your life expired three years from today, how would you live? What would you change? What steps would you take to leave a lasting legacy and an eternal impact? Would you go do more stuff, or would you do less stuff, just better?

I imagine that if you received this news, you wouldn't neglect discipling your children, your family, or your friends. You wouldn't waste time on frivolous, temporal arguments. The fact of the matter is that each one of us already has a clock running for the end of our time on earth, so we've passed the time to begin making these kinds of disciples. A Chinese proverb states, "The best time to plant a tree was twenty years ago. The second best time is today."

So it is with making disciples.

Let us leave a lasting legacy by starting today.

Chapter 4
COMMUNAL

*"Go, therefore, and make disciples of all nations, **baptizing them** in the name of the Father and of the Son and of the Holy Spirit, teaching them to observe everything I have commanded you. And remember, I am with you always, to the end of the age." Matthew 28:19-20*

When I was growing up, my dad and uncle loved to watch the Lone Ranger. This was an old Western TV show in which one Ranger was the last survivor of a group of six Texas Rangers. He wore a mask to conceal his identity as he traveled the West fighting for law and order. But the title of the show was misleading. The Lone Ranger was never alone. He rode a trusty horse named Silver and traveled with his friend named Tonto, who frequently helped him escape perilous situations. Even the Lone Ranger knew it was impossible to live alone.

Unfortunately, the idea Lone Ranger Christianity has infected the church. Some believers think they can live separate and apart from the local church when, in fact, it is impossible to grow as a Christian apart from the community of faith. Remember, the Church is not a place, but a people.

Ed Stetzer and Eric Geiger stated in their book *Transformational Groups*, "A call to discipleship and spiritual maturity is a call to biblical community. The call to discipleship is an invitation to hear and obey the voice of God. Also, a call to discipleship is a call to follow Jesus and be sent as a missionary to your community and world."[xix] Living isolated and alone is an unbiblical concept. God expects us to live communally with other believers for spiritual growth, encouragement, and accountability.

The writer of Hebrews explains why living in community is vitally important for a Christian's life:

> Therefore, brothers, since we have boldness to enter the sanctuary through the blood of Jesus, by a new and living way He has opened for us through the curtain (that is, His flesh), and since we have a great high priest over the house of God, let us draw near with a true heart in full assurance of faith, our hearts sprinkled clean from an evil conscience and our bodies washed in pure water. Let us hold on to the confession of our hope without wavering, for He who promised is faithful. And let us be concerned about one another in order to promote love and good works, not staying away from our

worship meetings, as some habitually do, but encouraging each other, and all the more as you see the day drawing near (Hebrews 10:19-25).

A Common Confidence in Christ

Have you ever wondered what it's like to enter the presence of a king or a queen? To stand in the halls of Buckingham palace waiting to visit the Queen of England for the very first time would be a nerve-wracking and humbling experience because of her persona and prestige. Now imagine standing before the God of the universe. The God who created you with His own hands. The God who numbered the hairs on your head and knit you together in your mother's womb. The God who set moons into orbit, galaxies into motion, and cellular mitosis into full swing. On what basis do you have the right to stand before such a God?

The writer of Hebrews tells us believers are able to *boldly* enter the presence of God because of the finished work of Christ on the cross of Calvary. Prior to Jesus' death, people were unable to enter into God's presence, but were separated by the curtains of the Holy Place and the Holy of Holies. Gentiles were not even allowed to stand in the same court as the Jews, much less approach the curtain surrounding the presence of God.

However, now because of the death, burial, and resurrection of Jesus Christ, we can approach God freely. The curtain that segregated us has been destroyed once and for all. Jesus' shed blood on the cross of Calvary satisfied the penalty that God imposed on sin. We do not approach God because of any merit we have achieved on our own, but only through the merit of Jesus' sacrifice on the Cross. We are now members of the family of God, joint heirs with Jesus, and inheritors of eternal glory. We are citizens of heaven, sojourning on the earth.

Every Christian who has professed faith in Christ is able to stand in the presence of God. What a privilege this is! Our confidence is based on nothing that we have done. It is based solely on the person and work of Jesus Christ.

A Clear Conscience and Common Confession

"Since we have a great high priest over the house of God, let us draw near with a true heart in full assurance of faith, our hearts sprinkled clean from an evil conscience and our bodies washed in pure water" (Hebrews 10:21–22).

Since the author of Hebrews is writing to a Jewish audience, he draws on images they would be readily familiar with in order to emphasize the death of Christ. Among the High Priest's many duties in the temple was overseeing the sacrifices. He was the one in charge of ensuring the blood of the sacrificial lambs was offered properly. He alone was able to enter the Holy of Holies. The problem with High Priests job was that it was never over. None of the sacrifices at the temple were good enough to cover the sins of the people forever; hence, sacrifices were perpetually offered to provide access to God.

This is why Jesus' death is essential—because His blood is sufficient to cover *any persons sins who put their faith in Him.* He is not just a High Priest. He is the Great High Priest who offered Himself as the sacrifice once and for all. As a result, everyone washed by His blood has unhindered access into the presence of Almighty God.

When the author of Hebrews mentions the "house of God," it does not imply a tabernacle or a temple made by human hands, for God's place of residence has changed. No longer does He confine His manifest glory on earth to an ark in a room. He dwells in the hearts of men and women who are born again and covered by the perfect sacrifice of His Son.

Therefore, it is with great joy that we should draw near to God in three ways:

With a sincere heart, meaning a *true* one. This is a heart that is focused and undivided, directed toward the Lord.

In full assurance of faith, meaning that the faith we have is not in man-made rituals but in God Himself. Hebrews 11:6 reiterates this point: "Now without faith it is impossible to please God, for the one who draws near to Him must believe that He exists and rewards those who seek Him."

With a clean conscience because of our consecrated, blood-washed bodies. Old Testament priests needed to consecrate themselves with blood and water in order to enter the presence of God, but we do not need to engage in this ritual any longer. The finished work of Christ on the cross cleanses us from all unrighteousness.

When a man named Chrysostom was brought before the Roman emperor, the emperor threatened him with banishment if he would not renounce Christ. Chrysostom replied, "You can't banish me, for this world is my Father's house."

"But I will slay you," said the Emperor.

"No, you cannot," said Chrysostom, "for my life is hid with Christ in God."

"I will take away your treasures."

"You cannot, for my treasure is in heaven and my heart is there."

"But I will drive you away from man and you shall have no friend left."

"You cannot, for I have a friend in heaven from whom you cannot separate me. I defy you, for there is nothing you can do to hurt me."[xx]

Chrysostom demonstrated precisely what it means to act in assurance of our faith. Remember Hebrews 10:23: "Let us hold on to the confession of our hope without wavering, for He who promised is faithful." Through His faith in God, Chrysostom was able to access God directly and tap into the hope that is found in Him.

The author of Hebrews wrote about this long before Chrysostom lived, but he did not stop at describing our newfound access to God; he goes on to give us a picture of how we should live by talking about our confession of hope. He summarizes the passage: we must actively believe in the face of any circumstance in life, death, riches, or poverty, knowing that the God who saves the believer through the sacrificial death of Christ has promised to never leave us.

John MacArthur tells the story of a young boy whose dad left him on a downtown corner one morning and told him to wait there until he returned in about half an hour. But the father's car broke down and he could not get to a phone. Five hours went by before the father managed to get back, and he was worried his son would be in a state of panic. But when the father got there, the boy was standing in front of the dime store, looking in the window and rocking back and forth on his heels. When the father saw him, he ran to him, threw his arms around him, and hugged and kissed him.

The father apologized and said, "Weren't you worried? Did you think I was never coming back?"

The boy looked up and replied, "No, dad. I knew you were coming. You said you would."[xxi]

In the same way, our Heavenly Father promised He will never leave or forsake us. Such a common confession bonds people together closer than brothers, for it is a connection that will last throughout eternity.

A Common Consideration for Others

What does this have to do with disciple-making? The author of Hebrews brings all of the previous statements to a point: "Let us be concerned about one another in order to promote love and good works, not staying away from our worship meetings, as some habitually do, but encouraging each other, and all the more as you see the day drawing near" (Hebrews 10:24-25).

In this text are two commands that simply cannot be disregarded: spur one another on and meet together. Both are indispensable in our walk as believers.

While these exhortations may seem disjointed and disconnected, they actually flow directly from one another. Notice the author does not give his audience a choice in whether they should care for one another; it is a direct order. How is it possible to promote good works and care for other believers if you only attend a 1-hour weekly worship service?

It's impossible.

A D-group offers the opportunity to live out the "one anothers" in the Bible. There are 59 "one anothers" found throughout the New Testament, including,

- Love one another. (John 13:34)
- Be in agreement with one another. (Rom.12:16)
- Accept one another. (Rom. 15:7)

- Instruct one another. (Rom. 15:14)

- Greet one another. (Rom. 16:16)

- Serve one another. (Gal. 5:13)

- Be kind and compassionate to one another. (Eph. 4:32)

- Submit to one another out of reverence for Christ. (Eph. 5:21)

- Admonish one another with all wisdom. (Col. 3:16)

- Encourage one another and build each other up. (1 Thess. 5:11)

- Be hospitable to one another. (1 Pet. 4:9)

- Confess your sins to one another and pray for one another. (James 5:16)

The Christian walk is one we simply cannot live out alone. Remember, it was born directly out of a Hebraic culture deeply entrenched in community. Every facet is expected to be lived together with like-minded individuals, spurring one another on to good works daily. Even a number of our prayers are communal! How strange would it be to pray in a group of believers, "My Father, Who is in heaven, hallowed be Your name"? Jesus, when instructing His disciples on how to pray, begins, "Our Father" (Matt. 6:9, emphasis mine).

So much of our lives are lived isolated and insulated from other believers. This is not the way Christ or the disciples of the early church encouraged their people to live. It is not the way Christianity is designed to function.

Worship with Other Believers

Hebrews 10:25 specifically references "worship gatherings," as the HCSB renders it. Meeting together is in one sense the weekly church service so many associate with Sunday mornings, but it more appropriately means meeting with other believers regularly for community and accountability.

The author offers a strong admonition to continue meeting together since some have apparently stopped. He actually uses the phrase "gather together" as a foreshadowing of the eschatological gathering of all of the saints at the second coming of Christ. This further meaning gains credibility from the end of the sentence: "As you see the day drawing near" (Heb. 10:25).

Because we are anticipating the final gathering of God's people, it makes sense to gather together now in preparation for that day. Our assembling on this earth is a picture of our assembling in Heaven. If gathering together with other believers isn't necessarily your cup of tea, think of how miserable heaven will be for you, standing shoulder-to-shoulder with people from every tribe, nation, and tongue, worshipping the

God of the universe forever! A true disciple of Christ seeks community with like-minded believers. D.L. Moody put it this way: "Church attendance is as vital to a disciple as a transfusion of rich, healthy blood to a sick man."[xxii]

Unity in the Community

Living as a believer is tough within a Christian community. It is *impossible* without it. An essential component you experience in a D-group that doesn't happen in the large gathering or even in a small group or Sunday school class is participation. In a group of three to six, there are no passive participants. The small numbers simply do not allow someone to sit in the back of the room without posing or answering a question.

As this group meets together, they grow together as well. The Jewish people called their gatherings *haverim*. In modern Hebrew, *haverim* means "friends." In Jesus' day, haverim were companions in study—they were dedicated members of the covenant community who immersed themselves in God's Word together.

Here is a line from the Babylonian Talmud that encapsulates this point: "Much have I learned from my teachers even more from my haverim, but from my disciples, most of all."[xxiii] The level of transparency, trust, and participation in our D-groups should foster a community of dedicated followers of Christ seeking to grow closer to Him as we grow together.

Another practice to include for developing close friendships is a one-on-one lunch meeting with each D-group participant. My current group set appointments with every member to meet individually for lunch throughout the year. The group of six men I'm currently leading will schedule six lunches over the course of a year to get to know each participant better. Ultimately, D-groups develop what I call 2 AM friends. These are close friends you can call at 2 AM with the full understanding they will answer the phone and be there in your time of need. It is one of the great benefits of being in a D-group.

The sustainability of the Church in the decades ahead will not be determined by the breadth of its members, but by the depth of its disciples. Depth is unearthed through trust and rapport with others. It's great that a weekly worship service may be attended by several thousand people, but the real question is: How many of those members are meeting together in discipleship for life-transformation?

Community was so important to Jesus that He lived communally with twelve men for three years. Ed Stetzer and Eric Geiger conclude, "We need to stop presenting community as just another option for the religious consumer and start presenting it as God's will for everyone. It should be seen as the reality of those within the church and the refuge for those without."[xxiv] To carry out the commands of Christ by caring for one another, we must avoid isolation at all cost.

D-groups are the solution.

Chapter 5
SCRIPTURAL

"Go, therefore, and make disciples of all nations,
baptizing them in the name of the Father and of
the Son and of the Holy Spirit, teaching them to
observe **everything I have commanded you.** *And*
remember, I am with you always, to the end of
the age." Matthew 28:19-20

During Bill Leslie's tenure as pastor of Lasalle
Street Church in Chicago, he felt as if his soul was
becoming a barren desert. His people's demands
were draining him spiritually. He didn't know what
to do about it.

While in this state of spiritual drought, he struck
up a conversation with a devout Christian woman
in his church. He told her he felt like a pump that
his people were constantly pumping dry. Straight

from her heart, she answered, "Didn't you volunteer to be pumped when you prayed to be used by the Lord? Don't ask your people to quit pumping. Drive your pump deeper. You need to get down to where there's water again."[xxv]

One of the biggest problems today is many Christians are drawing from an empty well. Burnout is a problem seen across many aspects of the Christian life from discipleship to pastoral ministry. The culprit may be the result of something simple: spiritual malnourishment. During those drought-inducing seasons, it is all the more crucial to drive the pump of faith deep into the Word of God and allow it to dwell richly in our lives.

The last element of the MARCS is the most important. Every D-group must be Scriptural. Being able to dig deeply into the Word is a privilege that has not been afforded to many Christians throughout history. A mantra of my life has been:

"Get into the Word until the Word gets into you." I do not say it to be cliché or blithe; rather, I'd like to demonstrate how I came to this conclusion from Scripture.

In his letter to the Colossians, Paul wrote: "And let the peace of Christ rule in your hearts, to which indeed you were called in one body. And be thankful. Let the word of Christ dwell in you richly, teaching and admonishing one another in all wisdom, singing psalms and hymns and spiritual songs, with thankfulness in your hearts to God. And whatever you do, in word or deed, do everything in the name of the Lord Jesus, giving thanks to God the Father through him" (Colossians 3:15-17).

A Heart Ruled by His Peace

Paul wrote something similar to the above passage when he encouraged the church at

Philippi; "And the peace of God, which surpasses every thought, will guard your hearts and minds in Christ Jesus" (Philippians 4:7).

The passage in Colossians instructs us to let the peace of Christ *rule* in our hearts. The New English Bible rendered this word "rule" as "arbiter." Though we do not use this word often in our speech, it portrays a vivid word picture that Paul is attempting to explain. He's borrowing an image from the Olympic arena by saying, "Let the peace of God be the referee in your heart." Have you yielded to the lordship of Christ? Frankly put, **when Christ rules your heart, peace reigns in your life**.

The peace of God is most often displayed on the mission field. I traveled with my friend David Platt and some others to train pastors in Southeast Asia in 2005 to a predominantly Muslim community. Adam, another man on the trip, was wearing a Christian t-shirt in the hotel lobby during breakfast one morning, prompting a man to approach unexpectedly.

The man asked if he could walk to our hotel room to share a video of Christians being persecuted for their faith in that country. After viewing the video, he encouraged us to keep a low profile while visiting the country. At that moment, the trip got real. Our first response was to get anxious or nervous. I began questioning whether we should be there at all—not out loud—but in my heart. Next, we got on our faces and prayed. We were reminded that God led us there. We were not there to promote ourselves; we were there to glorify God through training pastors. The moment we prayed, each of us was overcome by an unexplainable peace. We sensed the peace of God, stronger than the fear of death or persecution, course through our bodies like never before. It surpassed our understanding which screamed that we should be fearful for our lives.

In the midst of potential danger all around, I was reminded of this truth: **God's will never leads you to a place where His grace will not sustain you**. Our lives may be in danger or we may be facing peril because of His name, but our souls are safe and secure inside the providential hand of God.

This kind of peace only comes from one source. It cannot be obtained through acquiring material possessions, electing a favorite political candidate, achieving a particular socio-economic status, acquiring a desired job, or finding the perfect spouse. Perfect peace can only come from the One who gives perfect peace. Jesus said in John 14:27, "Peace I leave with you. My peace I give to you."

According to Romans 5:1, all believers in Christ Jesus have this peace with God, but not all believers experience the peace of God. We experience His peace by living according to His principles, engaging in prayer, and practicing His presence. Rest for restless hearts comes by accepting the peace that Christ freely offers.

A Mind Filed with His Word

Paul continues in Romans 5:16, "Let the Word of Christ dwell in you richly, teaching and admonishing one another in all wisdom, singing psalms and hymns and spiritual songs, with thankfulness in your hearts to God."

When Paul mentions "the Word of Christ," he envisions to the words Jesus spoke, the Scriptures. He was the Word who became flesh, dwelling among us, as the first chapter of John highlights. Interestingly, Paul uses that same word here as well.

To *dwell* means to live in or to reside in. It carries the idea of making something your home. Paul expects believers to allow the Word of God to take up residence in their lives. It should permeate every facet of a believer's existence. It should control every thought and govern each action. Paul says virtually the same thing in Ephesians 5:18: "Be filled with the Spirit." "Let The word of Christ dwell" and "be filled with the Spirit" are synonymous.

Paul then follows up with a pattern for how this should play out in the church: "Teaching and admonishing one another in all wisdom, singing psalms and hymns and spiritual songs, with thankfulness in your hearts to God."

Notice he does not delegate this task only to the clergy, pastors, elders, or worship leaders. He expects everyone in the body of Christ to teach, admonish, and sing psalms and hymns to one another. It is the fulcrum on which the entirety of the Christian life turns. It is the catalyst for revival. It was the basis of a reformation that occurred in Nehemiah 8 when Ezra read the Word of God publicly to the people after returning from exile. The people stood that day for six hours and listened, weeping, as they absorbed the Word of God into their hearts.

During the Dark Ages, Medieval Latin hymns sparked a revival among men in Monasteries. Furthermore, the Protestant Reformation was birthed with the words "Sola Scriptura," which means, "Scripture alone." The Reformation started when Martin Luther nailed his 95 Theses on the door of the Church of Wittenberg—95 ways the church had deviated from the teaching of the Word of God. **Simply put, revival happens when the people of God return to the Word of God.**

Walter Kaiser lamented about the sermons being delivered by many preachers today, saying "It is no secret that Christ's Church is not at all in good health in many places of the world. She has been languishing because she has been fed, as the current line has it, 'junk food'; all kinds of artificial preservatives and all sorts of unnatural substitutes have been served up to her. As a result, theological and Biblical malnutrition has afflicted the very generation that has taken such giant steps to make sure its physical health is not damaged by using foods or products that are harmful to their physical bodies."[xxvi]

Sadly, he is correct. Our modern problem is two-fold: junk food is being delivered from pulpits, and apathetic Bible readers are occupying the pews. Combined, these two factors present a significant problem that must be addressed. The solution to both of these issues is a simple one: be rooted, whether you are preaching, teaching, reading, acting, thinking, or anything else, in the Word.

A Life Lived for His Glory

In Colossians 3:17, Paul continues, "And whatever you do, in word or deed, do everything in the name of the Lord Jesus, giving thanks to God the Father through him."

When you build your life on the bedrock of Scripture, every word and deed should be pleasing to the Lord. Every single comment that passes through your lips, and every thought that enters your mind should be pleasing to the Lord. Every action includes the places you go, activities you engage in, jobs you take, items you purchase, hobbies you participate in, and websites you frequent. Even the way you treat your spouse when you are frustrated, and how you react to disappointing news should garner a Christ-honoring response.

The New Living Translation renders Colossians 3:17 this way: "And whatever you do or say, let it be as a representative of the Lord Jesus." There is simply no way to accomplish this in our own strength. Not one person is strong willed enough to fulfill this high standard. For this reason, it is absolutely imperative we soak our lives in the nourishment and instruction of Scripture. **What is on your mind comes out of your mouth**. This is why a daily diet of Scripture is a necessity.

What if every word that you said, every deed you enacted, and every thought that entered your mind was logged on a website for the world to see? On this website, your name is attached to every single thing you think and do. This would be horrifying for most, but let's take it one step further. What if all these actions and attitudes were attributed not to you, but to Jesus Christ? Every senseless act you or I carry out gets logged on the account of Jesus. Would this change your behavior? Would that cause you to pause before you act?

Each person who claims allegiance to Christ is joined to Him. Whether we like it or not, our actions are attached to His name. Every time you look at pornography, Jesus' name is attached to it. Every time you take advantage of someone, Jesus' name is attached to it. Every time you steal, Jesus' name is attached to it. Every time you abuse your spouse, Jesus' name is attached to it. Every time you sin, Jesus' name is attached to it.

For believers, there is no separation between the secular and the sacred. We cannot simply compartmentalize our lives between the church and the world. Our lives are always on display for everyone to see. These truths have specific applications to every believer's life, but most certainly to the life of a D-group. The D-group has the privilege of holding each member accountable to remain deeply rooted in the Word.

Three Ways a D-group Remains Faithful to Scripture

You wouldn't believe how many disciple-making processes use every resource but the Bible. While extra-biblical books support growth in a D-group, the textbook for every group is the Word of God. It is the bedrock for everything we do.

First, a D-group can remain faithful to Scripture by praying with expectancy to hear from God. This may seem simple, but a principle that will absolutely change the way you read the Bible is to pray before you begin. How often do we sit down and ask for enlightenment from God before we dive into His word? 1 Corinthians 2:14 says, "But the unbeliever does not welcome what comes from God's Spirit, because it is foolishness to him; he is not able to understand it since it is evaluated spiritually."

God is a God of clarity, not of confusion. He is a God of order and logic, so the result of a filling of the Holy Spirit is an understanding of the Word that God has given us. I sometimes hear from a charismatic brother or sister, "You Baptists are so boring in worship because you just sit around and study and listen to the Word. We prefer to sing and worship the Lord."

What a statement like this exposes is their desire for an *experience* when they come to worship. However, the highest form of worship for

111

the Jewish people was the study of God's Word. When the Jews gathered at the synagogue in the first century, they gathered to study the Bible. A typical service consisted of 45 minutes of reading the Word of God, followed by a 5-minute message. They sang in response to what they heard on the way home—not as the service began. Worship in song followed the truth of the Word; they let the Word of God mold their hearts rather than using a song to prepare them for what they were going to read.

Perhaps you're thinking, "I've never met Jesus personally. How can I sing about someone I don't know?" Peter answers this question by telling us the Word of God is as good as being there in person:

For we did not follow cleverly devised stories when we told you about the coming of our Lord Jesus Christ in power, but we were

112

eyewitnesses of his majesty. He received honor and glory from God the Father when the voice came to him from the Majestic Glory, saying, "This is my Son, whom I love; with him I am well pleased." We ourselves heard this voice that came from heaven when we were with him on the sacred mountain (2 Peter 1:16-20).

He lived with Jesus for three years. He heard Jesus' teaching directly from His mouth. He shared meals with Him, witnessed His miracles, walked on the surface of a roaring sea, saw His resurrected body, and *still* exclaims that we have something *more sure than all of this*: the Word of God. Preserved by faithful men and women throughout history, many suffered and died to ensure the survival of the Bible. Pray before you read this life-changing book and watch as your growth in the Christian life deepens exponentially.

Secondly, a D-group can remain faithful to Scripture is to read and journal the Scriptures daily. I remember during my time in seminary when classmates would tell me they didn't have a regular time of reading the Bible because they were so busy studying theological class textbooks. Hear this: **the last thing you want to do is read someone else's thoughts about Scripture in place of reading it for yourself**.

Since my wife Kandi and I lived an hour away from each other when we were dating, we talked on the phone late into the night on a regular basis. I looked forward to this time when I would get to call her at night all day long.

After dating for three and a half months, I knew it was time to share with her that I loved her. I was in Glorieta, New Mexico at the retreat center when Kandi arrived. That morning I went to the florist and purchased 12 roses. Before she arrived on the campus, I handed out roses to each college student working in the different departments. As we walked into the bookstore, someone reached out from behind the desk and handed her a rose. When we walked in the Chuckwagon, a restaurant on campus, someone reached out and handed her another rose. This happened again at the post office, the cafeteria, and at the high ropes course. One man even ran across the field with a rose in his hand, chasing us down in my vehicle. This happened a total of eleven times.

The final rose was placed on top of a mountain between a few rocks overlooking the valley. When we arrived, I directed her toward the last rose before reading aloud a letter I had written. The final phrase was, "These are all the reasons why I love you."

As you can imagine, that was a special time for me to share how I felt about her. But I want you to imagine what kind of impact I would have made if I had given her eleven roses, sent her up the mountain by herself, and had her meet a college student in my place. With the final rose in his hand, he read my letter to her for me. When he recited the final phrase "These are all the reasons why I love you" would it have been as impactful? Certainly not. Secondhand information always breaks down.

Unfortunately, many frequently hear from God this way. Rather than getting alone with Him and His Word, we crowd our time with the thoughts and interpretations of others. Do not get me wrong, there is a time and a place for reading books other people have written about Scripture. You are reading one now. However, it is no substitute for hearing directly from God Himself in the Bible.

If the only time you hear God's Word is from a pastor on Sunday morning or a devotional book after rising each day, you are depriving yourself. There is nothing better than waking up early, grabbing a cup of coffee, and cracking open the Word to feast on fresh manna for your soul.

Finally, a D-group can stay faithful to Scripture by memorizing verses weekly. In a culture filled with iPads, computers, notebooks, and Moleskins, the discipline of Scripture memory is a lost art. We can't remember seven-digit phone numbers anymore, much less Bible verses! Most believers offer the same excuse: "I can't memorize Scripture because my memory is horrible."

Frankly, if anyone should have been able to use that excuse, it was me. Months removed from a $180 a day heroin and cocaine addiction in

2003, my memory was worse than the ink retention rate on a burning piece of paper. (My testimony can be read in Chapter 1 of *Growing Up* and online at: **www.heisnotwhoyouthink.com**). My mother recalls an incident after rehab where I reached for a glass from the pantry before filling it with Coca-Cola. Two minutes into a conversation with her, I began reaching for another glass. As I was twisting the top off of the 2-liter Coke again, my mom interrupted me, pointing out that I'd already done that same thing two minutes prior.

There was a commercial some years back with footage of an egg in a frying pan. "This is your brain on drugs," it said. Frankly, the commercial is extraordinarily accurate. Years of self-induced stimulants had taken a toll on my ability to recall anything. So you can imagine how I felt when, during my first D-group, David Platt said, "We are going to memorize Romans 1 together."

"Cool," I said. "What verse?"

David responded: "The entire chapter."

It took me more than six months to memorize Romans 1, 2, and 8. Then, on Easter Sunday, a little over a year after being saved, my family gathered together for Easter. My family, every one of them was Catholic at the time, thought my relationship with Christ was another fad that would eventually fade, like my stints collecting baseball cards, playing guitar, working as a DJ, performing card tricks, or training for the UFC. As time passed that day, my personal apologetics began falling on deaf ears, so I resorted to something different: reciting the Word of God.

After the meal was eaten, I stood up before my entire family and simply said, "I have something that I want to share with you guys. 'Paul, a servant of Christ Jesus, called to be an apostle, set apart for the gospel of God...'" I reciting all three chapters from the book of Romans before them. Years later, they would all admit that one experience impacted them more than any sermon I had preached to them. At that moment, I was but a servant of God delivering the Word of God, empowered by the Spirit of God, and leaving the results to God. Eventually, my dad, mom, and sister would surrender their lives to Jesus Christ and follow through with baptism. No part of this story is something that I can take credit for. The Word did all the work.

If there is one thing that believers should be known for, it is being people of the Book. In a D-group, the Bible is the textbook. People who live by the Book will be governed by it, and will see as they align their lives to what It says, their relationship with God will grow exponentially.

How to HEAR from God

In order to digest more of the Word, I have developed a simple method. It's called H.E.A.R. journaling. The H.E.A.R. journaling method promotes reading the Bible with a life-transforming purpose. No longer will your focus be on checking off the boxes of a reading plan, your purpose will instead be to read in order to respond to God's Word.

The acronym H.E.A.R. stands for *Highlight*, *Explain*, *Apply*, and *Respond*. Each of these four steps contributes to creating an atmosphere to hear God speak. After settling on a reading plan and establishing a time for studying God's Word, you will be ready to H.E.A.R. from God.

For an illustration of this method, let's assume that you begin your time with God in the Book of 2 Timothy, and today's reading is the first chapter of the book. It may seem trite, but it is absolutely imperative that we seek God's guidance in order to understand His word (q Cor. 2:12-14). Every time we open our Bibles, we should pray the simple prayer that David prayed: "Open my eyes so that I may contemplate wonderful things from Your instruction (Word)" (Ps. 119:18).

After praying for the Holy spirit's guidance, open your notebook or journal, and at the top left corner, write the letter "H". This exercise will remind you to read with a purpose. In the course of your reading, one or two verses will usually stand out and speak to you. After reading the passage of Scripture, *Highlight* each verse that speaks to you by copying it under the letter "H." Write out the following:

- The name of the book
- The passage of Scripture

- The chapter and verse numbers that especially speak to you
- A title to describe the passage

This practice will make it easier to find the passage when you want to revisit it in the future.

After you have highlighted the passage, write the letter "E" under the previous entry. At this stage you will *Explain* what the text means. By asking some simple questions, with the help of God's Spirit, you can understand the meaning of a passage or verse. Here are a few questions to get you started:

- Why was the passage written?
- To whom was it originally written?
- How does it fit with the verses before and after it?

- Why did the holy Spirit include this passage in the book?

- What is He intending to communicate through this text?

At this point, you are beginning the process of discovering the specific and personal word that God has for you from His Word. What is important is that you are engaging the text and wrestling with its meaning.

After writing a short summary of what you think the text means, write the letter "A" below the letter "E." Under the "A," write the word *Apply*. This application is the heart of the process. Everything you have done so far culminates under this heading. As you have done before, answer a series of questions to uncover the significance of these verses to you personally, questions like:

- How can this help me?
- What does this mean today?
- What would the application of this verse look like in my life?
- What does this mean to me?
- What is God saying to me?

These questions bridge the gap between the ancient world and your world today. They provide a way for God to speak to you from the specific passage or verse. Answer these questions under the "A." Challenge yourself to write between two and five sentences about how the text applies to your life.

Finally, below the first three entries, write the letter "R" for *Respond*. Your response to the passage may take on many forms. You may write a call to action. You may describe how you will be different because of what God has said to you through His Word. You may indicate what you are going to do because of what you have learned. You may respond by writing out a prayer to God. For example, you may ask God to help you to be more loving, or to give you a desire to be more generous in your giving. Keep in mind that this is your response to what you have just read.

Notice that all of the words in the H.E.A.R. formula are action words: *Highlight*, *Explain*, *Apply*, and *Respond*. God does not want us to sit back and wait for Him to drop some truth into our laps. Instead of waiting passively, God desires that we actively pursue Him. Jesus said, "Keep asking, and it will be given to you. Keep searching, and you will find. Keep knocking, and the door will be opened to you" (Matt. 7:7).

Now What?

Understanding the MARCS of a disciple is only the beginning. Where are you on your discipleship journey? Are you a disciple? Are you making disciples? This is, after all the life Jesus called every believer to live and His plan to reach the world with the Gospel. Perhaps this book has sparked a desire in you to lead a D-group or find someone who will disciple you in the context of a D-group. As a pastor or church leader, maybe you feel the burden to return to the method Jesus modeled for every Christian. Replicate Ministries exists to equip the local church to make disciples who make disciple-makers. We would love to help you as you follow Jesus' command to make disciples. Visit **Replicate.org/MARCS** for everything you need to train leaders, launch D-groups, and build a discipleship pathway in your church.

The Growing Up Series

01 Growing Up. *Growing Up* is a practical, easy-to-implement system for growing in one's faith. It is a manual for making disciples, addressing the what, why, where, and how of discipleship. *Growing Up* provides you with transferrable principles for creating and working with discipleship groups, allowing you to gain positive information both for yourself and for others as you learn how to help others become better disciples for Christ.

02 Firmly Planted. Why is spiritual growth complicated? *Firmly Planted* is the second book in the Growing Up series. In biblical, practical, and simple terms, the book shares a roadmap for spiritual maturity. *Firmly Planted* addresses topics such as how you can be sure of your salvation, why your identity in Christ affects everything you do, how to overcome the three enemies that cripple a Christian's growth, a battle plan for gaining victory over temptation, and the indispensable spiritual discipline every believer must foster.

03 Bearing Fruit. *Bearing Fruit* is the third book in the Growing Up series. In this book, the reader will understand how God grows believers. Robby identifies seven places the word "fruit" is found in the bible: fruit of holiness, fruit of righteousness, fruit of soul-winning, fruit of the spirit, fruit of the praise, fruit of repentance, and fruit of giving. You will understand your role in the fruit bearing process of spiritual growth. *Bearing Fruit* is applicable for new and mature believers alike.

GROWINGUPSERIES.COM

128

Customized Equipping

When it comes to making disciples, there are as many strategies as there are ministry contexts. Our experienced team of disciple-makers are ready to equip your church in any context. By focusing in the scalable principles of Jesus' ministry, the Replicate team can help you develop the best strategy for your church. Sessions include:

- Laying a Foundation for Disciple-Making
- Framework for Healthy D-Groups
- Framework for Healthy Life Groups
- Devastating Effects of Not Making Disciples

Custom training available on request.
Contact info@replicateministries.org for more info.

REPLICATE.ORG

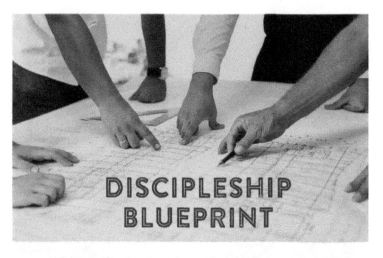

DISCIPLESHIP BLUEPRINT

Discipleship Blueprint is a two day experience that allows you to spend time in the context of a local church actively engaging in disciple-making. You'll have the opportunity to spend time with staff as well as walk alongside members as you:

1. Learn how to plan, formulate, and develop a disciple-making culture in your church and its ministries.

2. Study Jesus' and other historical models for making disciples.

3. Develop a comprehensive plan for raising up leaders in your church.

4. Learn how to navigate issues that arise in your D-Groups.

5. Participate in a D-Group led by an experience disciple-maker.

6. Consider principles and strategies for starting D-Groups and multiplying mature believers in your context when you return.

DISCIPLESHIPBLUEPRINT.COM

130

[i] Mike Breen and Steve Cockram, *Building a Discipling Culture* (Grand Rapids, MI: Zondervan Publishing House, 2009), Kindle Electronic Edition: Location 100-101.

[ii] Eugene H. Peterson, Working the Angels: The Shape of Pastoral Integrity (Grand Rapids, MI: William B. Eerdmans, 1987), 1.

[iii] Dallas Willard as quoted in Will Mancini (2013-09-24). *Innovating Discipleship: Four Paths to Real Discipleship Results* (Church Unique Intentional Leader Series) (Kindle Locations 163-164). Kindle Edition.

[iv] D. A. Carson, *Exegetical Fallacies* (Grand Rapids, MI: Baker Publishing Group: 1996), 33.

[v] Romans 10:14-15

[vi] 1 Peter 3:15

[vii] Dale Carnegie, *How to Win Friends and Influence People.* (New York: Simon and Schuster: 1981), 44.

[viii] Reggie McNeal, *Missional Renaissance: Changing the Scorecard for the Church.* (San Francisco: Jossey-Bassey: 2009), 20.

[ix] " from Cousins, Don and Judson Poling, *Discovering the Church: Becoming Part of God's New Community* (Grand Rapids: Zondervan, 1992), 50.

[x] Rod Handley, *Character Counts: A Guide for Accountability Groups* (Grand Island, NE: Cross Training Pub, 1999), 13.

[xi] Chuck Swindoll, *The Finishing Touch,* Dallas, Texas: Word, Inc., 1994.

[xii] The Jewish Study Bible (Oxford: Oxford University Press, 2004) Ecclesiastes 4:1-16.

[xiii] Source Unknown. www.bible.org/illustration/only-one-bible. Accessed 19 April 2016.

[xiv] Dietrich Bonhoeffer, *Life Together: The Classic Exploration of Christian in Community*. (New York: HarperOne: 2009), 112.

[xv]Phone conversation with Bill Hull, March 2013.

[xvi] Billy Graham, *The Holy Spirit: Activating God's Power in Your Life*. (Nashville: Thomas Nelson: 2000), 147.

[xvii]2 Timothy 2:1-2

[xviii] Herschel Hobbs, Discipleship Library, http://www.discipleshiplibrary.com/iea_om.php. Accessed 18 April 2016.

[xix] Ed Stetzer and Eric Geiger, *Transformational Groups*. (Nashville: B&H: 2014), 21.

[xx] Kevin Landis, *8 Seconds: The Cowboy Guide to Riding the Christian Life*. (Mustang, OK: Tate: 2007), p.120.

[xxi] MacArthur, John. *Strength For Today: Daily Readings for a Deeper Faith* (Wheaton, IL: Crossway, 1997), 60.

[xxii] George Sweeting, Who Said That? (Chicago, IL: Word Publishers, 1985), 127.

[xxiii] Taanit 7a.

[xxiv] Ed Stetzer and Eric Geiger, *Transformational Groups*. (Nashville: B&H: 2014), 21.

[xxv] Vernon C. Grounds "Drive the Pipe Deeper," Our Daily Bread. Sept. 29, 1996.

[xxvi]Walter Kaiser, *Toward an Exegetical Theology: Biblical Exegesis for Preaching and Teaching* (Ada, MI: Baker: 1998), 7-8.